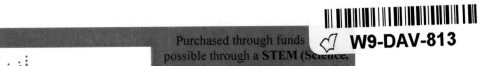

Thomas Edison
Incredible Inventor

written by Amanda Doering Tourville   illustrated by Reed Sprunger

Beginner Biographies

Content Consultant:
Paul Israel, Director and General Editor,
Thomas A. Edison Papers, Rutgers University

magic wagon

Text by Amanda Doering Tourville
Illustrations by Reed Sprunger
Edited by Holly Saari
Series design by Emily Love
Cover and interior production by Craig Hinton

Library of Congress Cataloging-in-Publication Data

Tourville, Amanda Doering, 1980-
  Thomas Edison : incredible inventor / written by Amanda Doering Tourville ; illustrated by Reed Sprunger
; content consultant, Paul Israel, director and general editor, Thomas A. Edison Papers, Rutgers University.
    pages cm. – (Beginner biographies)
  Audience: 4-10
  Includes bibliographical references and index.
  ISBN 978-1-61641-936-3
  1. Edison, Thomas A. (Thomas Alva), 1847-1931–Juvenile literature. 2. Inventors–United States–Biography-
-Juvenile literature. 3. Electrical engineers–United States–Biography–Juvenile literature. I. Sprunger, Reed,
illustrator. II. Title.
  TK140.E3T68 2013
  621.3092–dc23
  [B]   2012026516

Table of Contents

Science books were Thomas's favorite books to read.

Young Thomas Edison

Thomas Alva Edison was born on February 11, 1847, in Milan, Ohio. He was the youngest of seven children. When Thomas was seven, his family moved to Michigan. He soon started school, but he did not attend for long. His mother then taught him at home. Thomas kept learning on his own, too. He was smart and curious, and he loved to read.

Around age 12, Thomas started working to help earn money for his family. He took a job at a railroad. He sold candy and newspapers to train passengers.

Thomas kept teaching himself new things. He read when he wasn't working. He set up a laboratory in a train car. There, Thomas did science experiments.

As he grew up, Thomas continued to be interested in science.

Edison started working as
a telegrapher in 1863.

The Telegrapher

Edison soon learned to work the telegraph. At this time, telephones and the Internet did not exist. However, people could send each other messages by telegraph. Edison spent five years traveling around the Midwest working as a telegrapher.

Messages on telegraphs came in code. They were sent over wires using electricity. As a telegrapher, Edison decoded the messages and passed them along.

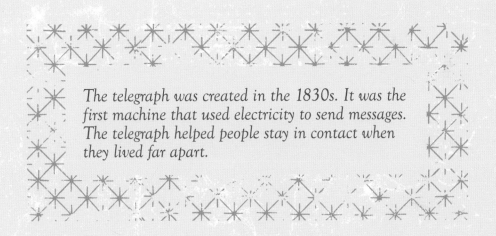

The telegraph was created in the 1830s. It was the first machine that used electricity to send messages. The telegraph helped people stay in contact when they lived far apart.

First Inventions

In 1868, Edison moved to Boston, Massachusetts. He spent a lot of time working on inventions. He hoped to sell them.

One of his first inventions was an electric vote recorder. Lawmakers could use the machine to cast their votes. It would make voting and counting votes much faster. But Edison's vote recorder did not sell. Edison learned from this. He would only invent things that were sure to sell.

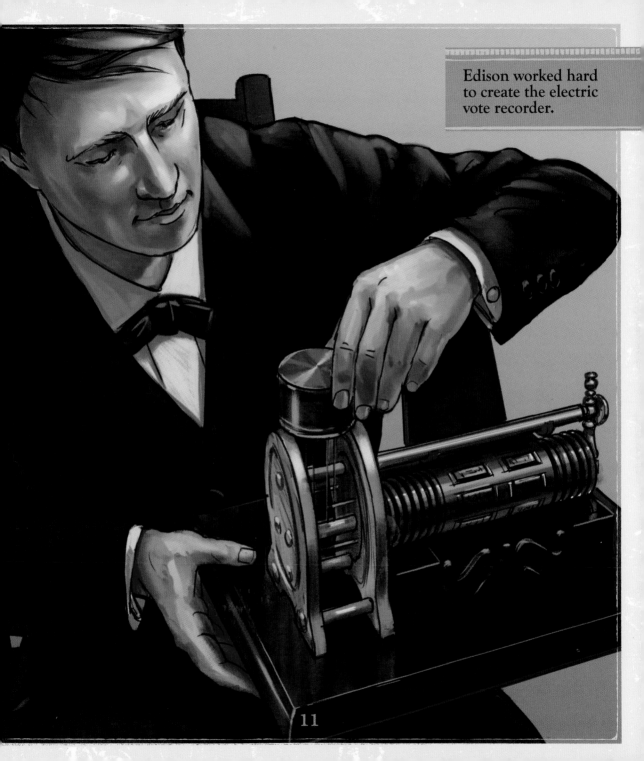

Edison worked hard to create the electric vote recorder.

11

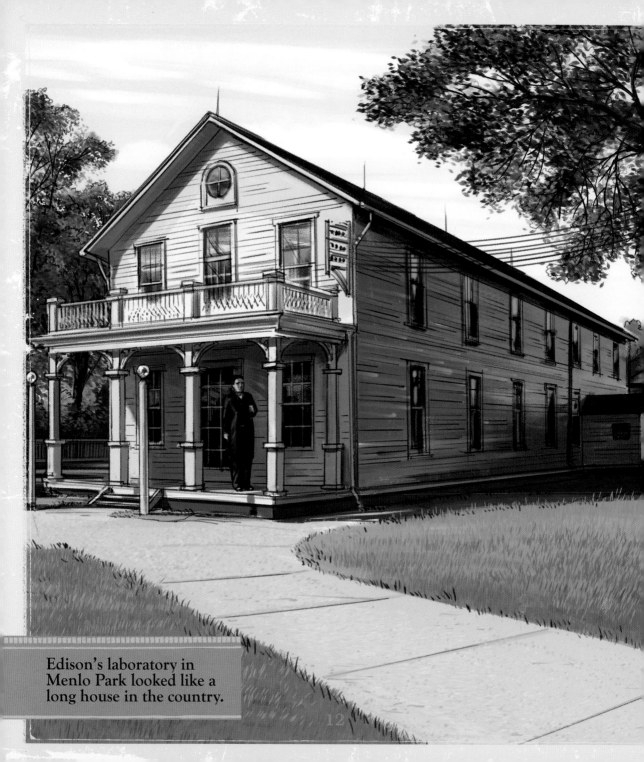

Edison's laboratory in Menlo Park looked like a long house in the country.

Over the next few years, Edison created new kinds of telegraphs. He was able to sell them. He used the money he made to build a small laboratory in Newark, New Jersey. A few years later, he built a larger one in Menlo Park, New Jersey. There, he continued his work on the telegraph. He worked on new inventions, too.

In 1871, Edison married Mary Stilwell. They had one daughter, Marion, and two sons, Thomas and William.

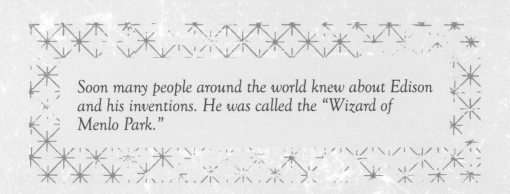

Soon many people around the world knew about Edison and his inventions. He was called the "Wizard of Menlo Park."

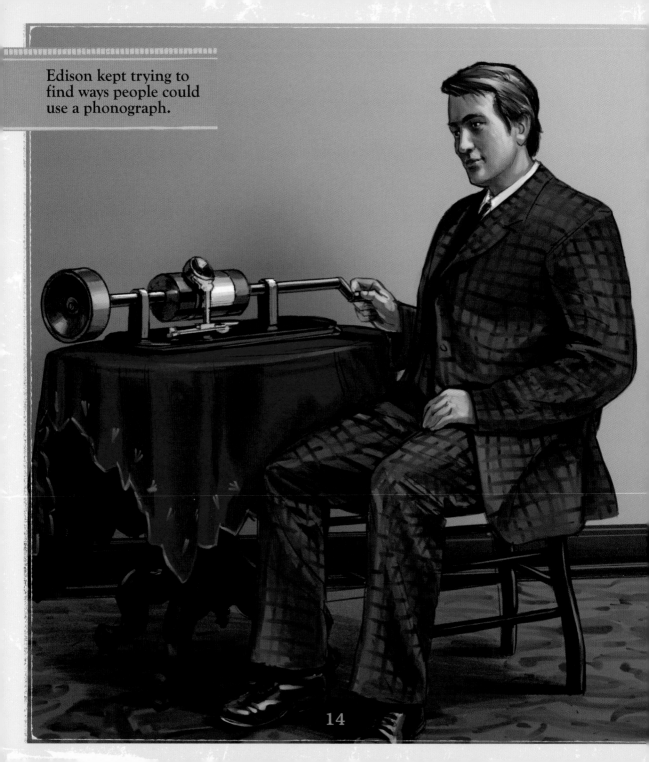

Edison kept trying to find ways people could use a phonograph.

14

The Phonograph

Edison did not plan his next invention. Alexander Graham Bell had invented the telephone in 1875. Edison had been working to improve the device, but his experiments led him in a new direction. In 1877, he invented the phonograph, or record player. It played sound recordings.

At first, people were excited about the phonograph. But then the excitement went away. People didn't see how the invention was helpful to them. It didn't become popular until several years later.

The Lightbulb

Edison's next project was a big one. In the 1870s, homes and businesses were lit using gas or oil lamps. Other inventors had created lightbulbs. But none were good enough for everyday use. Edison felt he could invent a better way to provide light.

In 1879, Edison created the first electric lightbulb for everyday use. It could light homes, streets, and businesses. But without electricity, few buildings could use Edison's invention. In 1882, he built the first electric power station. This power station provided light and power to one square mile (1.6 sq km) of New York City.

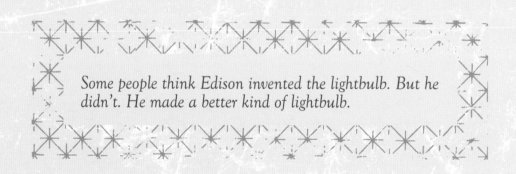

Some people think Edison invented the lightbulb. But he didn't. He made a better kind of lightbulb.

Edison's new lightbulb and power station changed how people lit their homes.

Edison and Mina had a daughter, Madeleine, and two sons, Charles and Theodore.

Life Changes

The mid-1880s brought many changes in Edison's life. His wife, Mary, died in 1884. In 1885, Edison met Mina Miller. Thomas and Mina married in 1886. They moved to West Orange, New Jersey.

Edison built a new laboratory in West Orange. This laboratory was much larger than the one in Menlo Park. It also included a factory. Here, many copies of Edison's products could be made for sale.

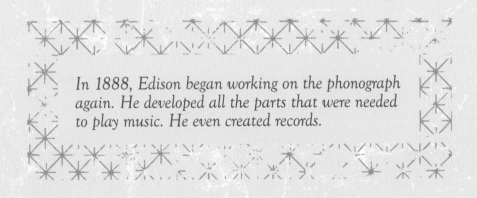

In 1888, Edison began working on the phonograph again. He developed all the parts that were needed to play music. He even created records.

Failed Inventions

Many of Edison's inventions were successful, but some were not. Edison saw an opportunity in iron ore, a rock that has valuable iron inside it. He opened his own mine in New Jersey. There, he invented a way to mine ore with very little metal in it.

Edison spent ten years on the project. He also spent $2 million dollars of his own money. But the discovery of better iron ore dropped the price of the metal. Edison was forced to close his mine because he did not make money on it.

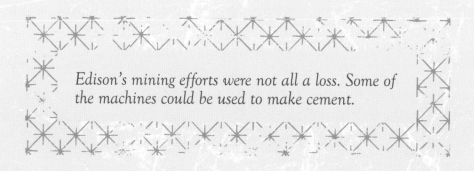

Edison's mining efforts were not all a loss. Some of the machines could be used to make cement.

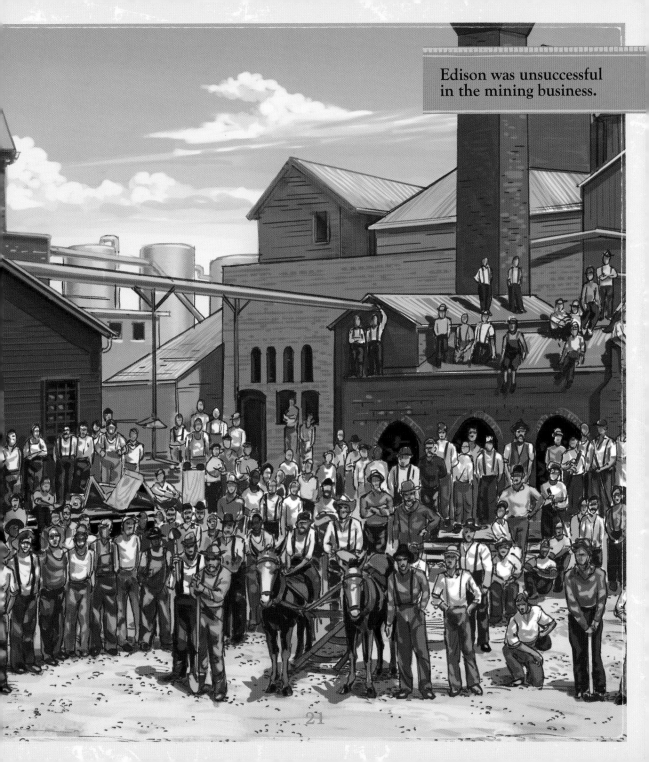

Edison was unsuccessful in the mining business.

For his next invention, Edison worked closely with a member of his staff named W. K. L. Dickson. In 1891, the two men invented a movie camera. To watch a movie, people had to look through a kinetoscope. This looked like a large cabinet with a hole on top. Edison had a studio built at his laboratory. It made many movies. But Edison spent much of his time working on other projects.

Edison did not think the kinetoscope was very important. He thought of it as a toy.

Thomas A. Edison Inc.

By 1911, Edison was spending less time inventing and more time running all his companies. They were becoming hard to manage. So Edison combined them all into one. Thomas A. Edison Inc. was created.

Edison still spent time improving some of his inventions, like the phonograph. And he created new ones, like better batteries.

Employees put together the new phonographs.

25

Edison helped the U.S.
Navy during World War I.

World War I

In 1915, the U.S. government asked Edison for help. The United States was preparing for World War I. Edison worked with other inventors and scientists. They thought of ways to help the U.S. military fight better. During this time, Edison worked on a machine that would find submarines. When the war ended in 1918, he returned to his own company.

Thanks to Edison, people can still do many activities when it is dark outside.

Final Years

During his last years, Edison's health was poor. He died on October 18, 1931. He was 84 years old. The whole nation mourned Edison's death. His funeral was on October 21. That night, people everywhere turned down their lights for a short time. In the darkness, they remembered the man who had helped light their homes. They honored one of the greatest inventors of all time.

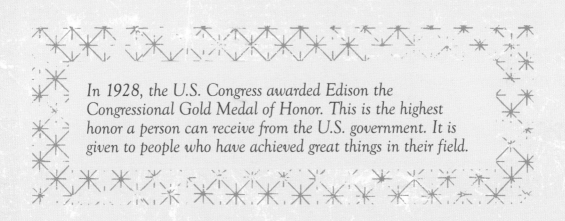

In 1928, the U.S. Congress awarded Edison the Congressional Gold Medal of Honor. This is the highest honor a person can receive from the U.S. government. It is given to people who have achieved great things in their field.

FUN FACTS

✦ During his lifetime, Edison had 1,093 U.S. patents! A patent allowed him to be the only person who could make or sell that particular invention.

✦ Edison lost most of his hearing at a young age. He was nearly deaf when he died.

✦ The words of the nursery rhyme "Mary Had a Little Lamb" were the first sounds ever played on Edison's phonograph.

TIMELINE

1847 Thomas Alva Edison was born on February 11 in Milan, Ohio.

1863 Edison began working as a telegrapher.

1868 Edison invented the electric vote recorder.

1877 Edison invented the phonograph.

1879 Edison created the electric lightbulb for everyday use.

1882 Edison opened the first electric power station in New York City.

1891 Edison and W. K. L. Dickson invented a movie camera.

1915 Edison began working for the U.S. government during World War I.

1931 Edison died on October 18.

GLOSSARY

code—a system of special words, letters, or numbers used instead of regular words to send messages.

decode—to turn something written in code into an understandable message.

device—a piece of equipment that does a certain job.

laboratory—a place where scientific experiments are performed.

passenger—a person, other than the driver, who travels in a vehicle.

submarine—a naval ship designed to operate underwater.

telegraph—a device that uses electricity to send coded messages over wires.

telegrapher—a person who runs a telegraph.

World War 1—from 1914 to 1918, fought in Europe. Great Britain, France, Russia, and the United States, and their allies were on one side. Germany, Austria-Hungary, and their allies were on the other side.

LEARN MORE

At the Library

Berger, Melvin, and Gilda Berger. *What Makes the Light Bright, Mr. Edison?* New York: Scholastic, 2006.

Carlson, Laurie. *Thomas Edison for Kids: His Life and Ideas: 21 Activities.* Chicago: Chicago Review, 2006.

Colbert, David. *Thomas Edison.* New York: Simon & Schuster, 2008.

Frith, Margaret. *Who Was Thomas Alva Edison?* New York: Penguin, 2005.

On the Web

To learn more about Thomas Edison, visit ABDO Group online at **www.abdopublishing.com**. Web sites about Edison are featured on our Book Links page. These links are routinely monitored and updated to provide the most current information available.

INDEX